Rumble in the Jungle

To Tigger
G.A.

For my Mum and Dad
D.W.

ORCHARD BOOKS
96 Leonard Street, London EC2A 4XD
Orchard Books Australia
Unit 31/56 O'Riordan Street, Alexandria, NSW 2015
1 84362 066 9
First published in Great Britain in 1996
First paperback edition published in 1998
This edition published in 2002
Text © Purple Enterprises Ltd 1996
Illustrations © David Wojtowycz 1996
The right of Giles Andreae to be identified as the author and
David Wojtowycz as the illustrator of this work has been asserted by them
in accordance with the Copyright, Designs and Patents Act, 1988.
A CIP catalogue for this book is available from the British Library
2 4 6 8 10 9 7 5 3 1
Printed in Dubai

Rumble in the Jungle

Giles Andreae

Illustrated by
David Wojtowycz

ORCHARD BOOKS

There's a rumble in the jungle,
There's a whisper in the trees,
The animals are waking up
And rustling the leaves.

The hippo's at the waterhole,
The leopard's in his lair,
The chimpanzees are chattering
And swinging everywhere.

Some animals are frightening,
And some are sweet and kind,
So let's go to the jungle now
And see who we can find . . .

munch   munch

Chimpanzee

oo oo

It's great to be a chimpanzee

Swinging through the trees

And if we can't find nuts to eat

We munch each other's fleas!

R r

Lion

The lion's the king of the jungle
Just listen how loudly he roars!
Every animal quivers
And shudders and shivers
As soon as he opens his jaws.

Elephant

It's great to be an elephant
All big and fat and round,
And wander through the jungle
Just elephing around.

munch

Zebra

I could have been grey like a donkey
Or brown like my cousin the mule,
But instead I've got stripes
Which my ladyfriend likes,
As they make me look handsome and cool.

Snake

The boa constrictor's a slippery snake
Who slithers and slides round his tree,
And when tasty animals wander too close
He squashes them slowly for tea.

Ssss

Giraffe

Some animals laugh

At the gangly giraffe

But I hold my head up and feel proud,

I really don't care

When my head's in the air

And my cheek's getting kissed by a cloud.

Hippopotamus

Hello, I'm a big happy hippo
I sleep in the sun to get hot,
And when I'm not sleeping
I mooch in the mud,
Which hippos like doing a lot.

Crocodile

When animals come to the river to drink
I watch for a minute or two,
It's such a delight
To behold such a sight
That I can't resist chomping a few.

Rhinoceros

The ravenous rhino
Is big, strong and tough,
But his skin is all baggy and flappy,
Which means that there's plenty
Of room for his lunch,
And that makes him terribly happy.

Gazelle

No-one can run half as quickly as me
The galloping, gorgeous gazelle,
I can leap up so high
That my horns touch the sky,
And I'm awfully pretty as well.

Gorilla

The gorilla is big, black and hairy
And the thing that he likes to do best
Is to look all ferocious and scary
And wallop his giant great chest.

pat

pat

Leopard

If you meet a hungry leopard
Prowling through the night,
Make sure you call him 'Sir'
And be incredibly polite.

Tiger

Beware of the terrible tiger
You don't always know when he's near,
But his eyes shine like lights
Through the blackest of nights,
And his growl makes you tremble with fear.

Grrr

The night has started falling
But the jungle never sleeps,
The vultures circle slowly
While the leopard softly creeps.

And if you listen quietly
You might just hear the growl
Of a hungry pair of panthers,
Who are still out on the prowl.

The lions and their little cubs
Are sleeping in their den,
So let's leave them till tomorrow
When we'll visit them again.